Around Taunton

IN OLD PHOTOGRAPHS

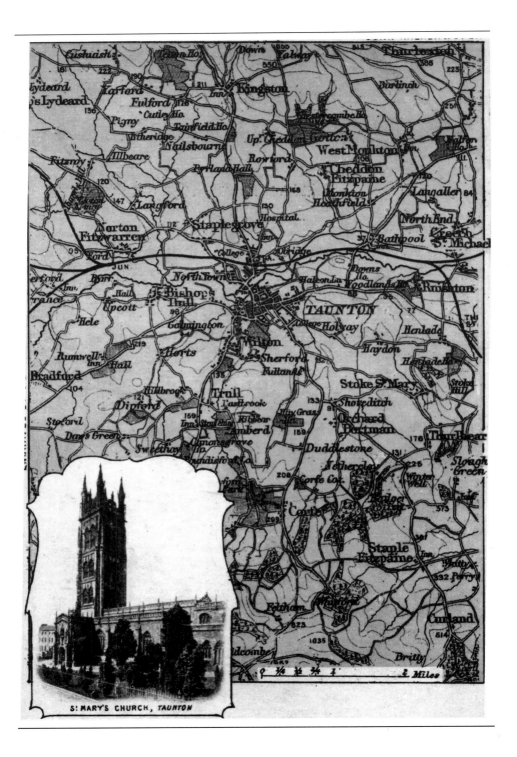

S: MARY'S CHURCH, TAUNTON

Around Taunton

IN OLD PHOTOGRAPHS

Collected by NICK CHIPCHASE

A Budding Book

First published in 1993 by Alan Sutton
Publishing Limited

This edition published in 1998 by Budding Books,
an imprint of Sutton Publishing Limited
Phoenix Mill · Thrupp · Stroud · Gloucestershire
GL5 2BU

I should like to dedicate this book to the pioneer
photographers who travelled far and wide in
pursuit of their pictures. Without their early
endeavours books such as this could not exist.

A catalogue record for this book is available from
the British Library

ISBN 1-84015-029-7

Typesetting and origination by
Sutton Publishing Limited.
Printed in Great Britain by
WBC Limited, Bridgend, Mid-Glamorgan.

Contents

Introduction

Within ten miles of Taunton, in the fertile belt of rich farmland that surrounds the county town, are some forty parishes. Life in the villages within these parishes has changed considerably over the last one hundred and twenty years and the aim of this selection of old photographs is to document some of the changes. The scope of the book is such that only those villages that would look to Taunton as their nearest town are included.

Although the whole area is known as Taunton Deane, I have used this heading only to cover the villages that are closest to the north and south of Taunton. This group includes Trull, Galmington, Wilton, Shoreditch, Stoke St Mary, Hatch Beauchamp and West Hatch. On the outer limits of this area are the villages of Halse and West Monkton. Villages that are situated westward, along the River Tone, follow in Section Two and these include Norton Fitzwarren, Hillfarrance, Bradford on Tone and the general area around Bishops Hull. Section Three follows the same river in an easterly direction and includes Creech St Michael, Ruishton and Bathpool. Where the River Tone enters the flatlands on the perimeter of Sedgemoor I have included the villages of Section Four, North Curry, Stoke St Gregory, Curry Mallet and Wrantage. Sections Five and Six include villages on the flanks of the Quantock and Blackdown Hills which border the Vale of Taunton Deane. To the north of the town lie Kingston St Mary, Bishops Lydeard, Combe Florey and Lydeard St Lawrence, while to the south lie Pitminster, Blagdon Hill, Corfe and Staple Fitzpaine.

Agriculture and related industries had been the major source of employment in the rural areas around Taunton for centuries. This had usually been carried on under the paternal eye of the wealthy landowners but the first few decades of this century saw the break up of the great landed estates, with many properties being transferred to individual private ownership. The Lethbridge Estate at Bishops Lydeard was dispersed in 1913, the Manor of Halse lands were auctioned off in 1939, and others, including the properties of the Viscount Portman, have followed suit.

Farming has, over the years, come to rely much less upon manpower. But in the nineteenth century agricultural labour was the commonest form of employment. Many were itinerant workers with large families moving from farm to farm and living in tied cottages. Long hours were worked in the fields but, generally, good health prevailed and infant mortality was far lower than in the cities.

The Yard(e) family are a typical West Country family. They came into Somerset from Devon via Staple Fitzpaine in the fifteen and sixteen hundreds. Initially owning property in the village, by 1700 the family had dispersed right across the farming villages of West Hatch, Curland, Pitminster and Hatch Beauchamp. The families were generally large so that by 1800 much of the property had become dispersed and many family members were working the land in the Taunton area. My own great grandfather, Harry Yard of West Hatch (1858–1930), had eleven children, and he himself was one of a brood of twelve. By their twelfth birthday most of the male children were working the land and, needless to say, adult literacy was not high. The young women were often engaged in cottage industries such as glove making or helped the men in the fields.

Mrs Sarah Blackmore of Creech St Michael, aged 90 when interviewed by the *Gazette* in 1921, was rather scathing in her attitude towards her modern counterparts. 'In my day,' she began, 'the women used to go into the fields and on the land to work. Wearing an old skirt and with my sleeves turned up, not for show like the maidens of nowadays, I have worked all day in the cornfields under a blazing sun. Bless your heart, women don't work in the present age.' Mrs Blackmore's final comment on a rougher and simpler Somerset is perhaps even more relevant today. She says with a deep sigh, 'Working people may be better off nowadays. They certainly make much more money and wear clothes we never dreamed of. But they don't enjoy life like we did. They haven't got such good health and they ain't anything near as happy.'

Many of the photographs in this book do, perhaps, show a simpler and more picturesque Somerset but we can never know how close they are to the complete truth. The visiting photographer was a rarity in rural parts. He picked nice bright days and avoided many of the muddier roads. The local folk had time to put on their Sunday best and parade in the street. We rarely have a glimpse of them at work. We see pretty thatched cottages but hardly ever their squalid and dark interiors. Our ancestors in the country had no running water, electricity or flush toilets. Even countryfolk of my own generation remember a childhood that included tin baths in front of a coal fire. (We often shared the same water.) A trip to the toilet usually involved a trek to the hut at the bottom of the garden. Without knowing the hardships of an earlier age how can subsequent generations appreciate the finer things in life that civilization has bestowed upon them?

Apart from changes associated with working and living conditions the greatest force for change has been the development of transportation. We have suffered the good and the bad as a result of these changes. Mobility has broadened the mind and increased opportunity and modern transportation has taken the drudgery out of travel; but this goes hand in hand with the destruction of local communities and their traditional ways of life. Some villages have, literally, been cut in half by road 'improvements', while others have been swamped by industrial and urban development due to their proximity to the main arterial routes.

Closely following upon the development of the canals came the railway, eventually leading to all four points of the compass with the centre at Taunton.

Many of the villages were close to a local station. Despite this the system of horse-drawn carriers prevailed until after the First World War, with most villages serviced by carriers on regular routes leading into Taunton. A resident of Stoke St Mary recorded that 'It cost a whole shilling to go by Mrs Kerton of Rattlepot Lane's cart and then you had to get out and walk up the hills.' Motor transport in the form of buses and private cars finally killed off the business.

The motor car appeared on local roads shortly before 1900. Their worth was proved by a 1,000 mile endurance rally that year. Many local dignitaries bought their first car in the initial decade of this century and several Taunton dealers were well established by 1914. Some of the cars seen in the photographs no doubt belong to the photographer. He would have chugged into the centre of the village and aroused the curiosity of the local children who happily posed for the picture. By the beginning of the 1920s motor transport was commonplace but the rural simplicity of life in the village was, perhaps, already destroyed by the greatest social upheaval this century, the First World War.

When such a small area is under consideration it is very difficult to present a complete picture of life in the village, as we have already discovered. So much remains unrecorded and the photographs that survive number but a few hundred. We have to rely mainly on the dozens of commercial photographers who usually liked to present a jolly village scene or record the local places of worship. As with the cities and towns the points of interest are usually incidental, the transport, the shop windows and the fashions. Many buildings are much the same today as they were fifty years ago. Contemporary photographers would do well to note that the people, the buses and motor cars in today's scene are going to fascinate those in years to come.

This volume and its companion, *Taunton in Old Photographs*, have provided over five hundred glimpses of life in this small corner of Somerset. The author hopes that his efforts have given readers a lasting view of times gone by, stirred the memories of older generations and shown newcomers that we have a heritage to be proud of.

Nick Chipchase, 1993

SECTION ONE
Taunton Deane

All Saints' church and the schoolhouse, Trull, _c._ 1860. At this time the church had·a stucco covering. The junction to Mill Lane is in the foreground. The cottage, which later became the author's family home, was re-structured sometime before 1905.

Trull village, possibly by the photographer Robert Gillo, *c.* 1880. The fields in the foreground are now occupied by Glencoe Terrace. The old schoolhouse (right) was built around 1755 and demolished in 1886. The photograph, the first collected by the author, was found in an empty cottage in Mill Lane in the 1960s.

Trull church and village, *c.* 1904. The gate to the school playground is on the right. (M. Cooper)

A view of Trull church and the old 'Poor Houses' in Mill Lane, *c.* 1903. The thatched cottage was demolished to extend the churchyard in 1904 and the remaining tiled cottages were removed around 1966. (Wykeham)

Interior view, All Saints' church, Trull, showing the fine rood-screen and pulpit, *c.* 1910. The bench ends are of particular note, one of them being dated 1510. (Frith)

The old stocks in Trull churchyard beneath a large yew tree. Harry Whale, master of Trull School until 1911, is buried under the same tree. It is not known why some stocks have an odd number of holes. (Frith)

The old oak tree in Trull Meadow, *c.* 1910. With the schoolmaster 'Daddy' Whale are: Ivor Carpenter, Emily Cross, Elsie Doble, Ernest Ebsary, Alice Flower, ? Greedy, Reg Hutchings, Gladys Hyman, Harry, Albert and Bill Melhuish, Ted Oakes, Doris Poole, Fred Rowsell, ? Sainsbury, Winnie Shires, Sybil Silk, Vera Sparks, Elsie Warren, Annie and Bessie Wide, Dorothy Wiginton. Harry Whale was master at Trull School for forty years.

Trull School, *c.* 1904. It was built in 1875 and enlarged in 1876 to teach 160 children. Subsequent developments have since doubled the size of the school.

Rose Cottage, Staplehay, home of William and Sarah Mutter, *c.* 1920. In the foreground are two of the author's uncles, Charles and Albert Yard.

Outside Rose Cottage, *c.* 1930. The driver is Mr Shire and the two ladies are Florence Cartwright and Sarah Mutter.

Trull AFC. A note on the back of the photograph refers to a boy called Pocock but none of the other players are named.

Clearing up flood damage at Trull, after the worst flooding in the village in living memory in July 1968. In Mill Lane a tractor and its driver were swept away but fortunately he was rescued by the fire brigade. (Author)

Old cottages on the Dipford Road at Trull, *c.* 1905. The rifle club opened opposite here in 1910.

Eastbrook, *c.* 1905. Eastbrook lies in the parish of Pitminster although it is considered by the locals to be part of Trull village. On the right is Eastbrook Lodge at the head of the drive to Eastbrook House.

Trull post office, *c*. 1910. Malcolm Long, sub-postmaster, is in the garden.

Post office and village shop, Trull, *c*. 1904. Albert Bull (extreme left) is the sub-postmaster, a position he combined with his trade as a plumber and glazier. The shop was run by Jane Johns.

Trull village, *c.* 1908. The author's family home stands on the corner of Mill Lane, but the railings were removed 'for the war effort'. Top left is the men's club building which was opened in 1896. The topiary peacock still exists.

A more distant view of Trull village, *c.* 1910. The cottages on the right were removed in the 1950s and replaced by modern brick houses.

The opening of Trull miniature rifle range on the Dipford Road, 28 March 1910. During the First World War free use of the electrically lit range was available to aid recruiting. Over seventy former members of the club entered the armed forces.

Members posing among the targets at the miniature rifle range. The targets were drawn back to the firing shelter along a small railway track. Robert Connett is standing in the centre. Rifle ranges were popular in the early 1900s, the one at Taunton opening in the Drill Hall in September 1906.

The opening of the Baptist chapel at Comeytrowe, 27 July 1895. Built of red brick with Bath stone facings by Mr Potter of Taunton, the cost of construction was borne by Mr Thomas Penny. Mr Facey had supplied the land at nominal cost and Mr Charles Allen had collected subscriptions for the furnishings. The opening ceremony was conducted in a marquee supplied free of charge by W. and A. Chapman of Taunton. The sermon was preached by the Revd Newnam of Yeovil. The first nonconformist chapel to be opened in the parish, it was converted to a private house in the early 1970s. (M. Cooper)

Fairview Terrace and Wild Oak Lane, Trull, *c.* 1910. The terrace was built in the early 1800s by Henry Mockridge who also built Southview Terrace. In the centre is Chantry Cottage, formerly known as the Church Cottage.

Wild Oak Lane and Glencoe Terrace, Trull, *c.* 1925.

The wooden post office at Trull, erected *c.* 1908. It had formerly belonged to the vicar who built it as a study at the old vicarage near Queen's College. The placard referring to a massacre by the Turks possibly dates this scene to the time of the Balkan Wars of 1912–13. The motor car belonged to Arthur Eastwood of Leigh Court.

Ramshorn Bridge and Galmington Fields, *c.* 1903. This would have been the site of Taunton's airport if a 1930s proposal had been accepted. West Somerset Gliding Club opened in Musgrove Field in 1931. (Wykeham)

Ramshorn Bridge, *c.* 1905. An Edwardian girl poses prettily on the archway. The little bridge still stands but on dry ground because the river has been diverted. (Frith)

Galmington village in quieter times, *c.* 1905. The Galmington Inn, now the Shepherds Rest, stands in the background. Farm labourers occupied the row of thirteen extremely primitive cottages on the right. These one-up-one-down houses with outside wash-houses were known as The Rank or The Court. Now largely demolished, their backs remain to form the lower garden wall of the Manor House. Robert Shattock stands in the gateway to his shop on the left.

Galmington, 1930. This old cottage stood on the corner of Comeytrowe Lane and Galmington Road, and is typical of the many village properties that were demolished between the wars. Mrs Hartland, seen here in the garden, and her family were moved to a new council house in 1934 when their roof became unsafe.

Robert Shattock's grocery shop at Galmington, c. 1906. This was demolished around 1960, together with about seven other cottages, to make way for the new post office and shops.

Galmington, 1908. The floral arch was erected at the end of Comeytrowe Lane to celebrate the wedding of Miss Dorothy Edwards, the local Sunday school teacher, to Mr Harry Thomas of Tangier House. The ceremony was conducted at St George's church, Wilton, by the Revd J.M. Bastard. Jewells Farm in the background was subsequently replaced by more modern houses.

Two views of Sherford Bridge on the footpath from Trull to Taunton. The earlier view (below), by Francis Frith, dates to around 1900, the later, by Chapman of Dawlish, to around 1910. The ivy on Bridge House has gained a much greater hold. The stream beyond the bridge at this time formed part of the boundary of the Borough of Taunton.

Shoreditch, on the main road from Taunton to Corfe, *c.* 1906. The card was sent by Alice, who lived at Octon Lodge, the large building on the right. (Cox)

Stoke St Mary village, *c.* 1905. The building in the distance is the Half Moon Inn. The Methodist chapel, right, was erected in 1825. (Abraham)

Hatch Beauchamp, *c.* 1880. Charles Chard awaits the imminent arrival of his famous brother, John, at Hatch Rectory. (Charles was rector at Hatch from 1885 to 1911.) Lt. John Rouse Merriott Chard of the Corps of Royal Engineers was born near Plymouth in 1847 and arrived at Rorkes Drift, aged thirty-one, with no previous experience of active service. On 22 January 1879 Lt. Chard, aware of an impending Zulu attack, ordered the fortification of Rorkes Drift. After a mass colonial desertion only 139 men were left to defend the garrison; of these 104 were fit but only 80 were combatants. The Zulu army repeatedly attacked the post for twelve hours but the British soldiers refused to yield. At the end of the battle the British had sustained twenty-seven casualties but the Zulus probably lost as many as five hundred men. For the gallant defence of Rorkes Drift eleven men, including Lt. Chard, were awarded the Victoria Cross, the most ever awarded for any single action in British military history. Lt. Chard received an accelerated promotion to brevet-major and eventually rose to the rank of colonel. Only ten months after this promotion he died, at the age of 50, from cancer of the tongue. He was buried at Hatch church on 1 November 1897. (M. Blizard)

Hatch Beauchamp, *c.* 1910. The gateway in the background leads to Hatch Court. Postcards marked JFB were produced by James Bridel who also ran the garage and cycle repair shop in the village. (J.F. Bridel)

Hatch Beauchamp post office, next to the Hatch Inn, *c.* 1904. In the garden is sub-postmaster William Marks with his two children, Jim and Eva. (Fisher)

Tytherleigh's stores, Hatch Beauchamp. The news of Togo's Fleet on the placards dates this scene to 1904 or 1905, during the Russian–Japanese conflict. Mr Tytherleigh's daughters went to Bishop Fox's School in Taunton by train. The site is now the village post office.

Hatch Beauchamp Public Elementary School, c. 1905. It catered for seventy children and was run by Alice Rich. The children had no playground and used to play on the railway embankment opposite the school.

The funeral procession of Revd Edward Curtis, pastor of the Baptist church at Hatch Beauchamp for thirty-eight years, who died in February 1907 aged 72. The procession passes a local shop whose blinds are drawn as a mark of respect.

Hatch Court, *c.* 1905. Between the wars this was the home of Lt.-Col. Hamilton Gault MP, president of the Taunton and West Somerset Gliding Club. (M. Cooper)

Hatch Beauchamp, *c.* 1904. Henry Fry's Hatch Inn is on the left. The gateway, right, leads into Mrs Raban's Beauchamp Lodge. (M. Cooper)

Hatch Baptist chapel, *c.* 1905. This chapel was built in 1783. According to some sources, teaching of the Baptist faith in Hatch began as early as 1630. (M. Cooper)

Hatch Beauchamp, with the junction of Bickenhall Lane on the right, *c.* 1904. The long thatched cottage in the centre (now tiled) is Perris Farm, which is said to be one of the oldest buildings in the village. (M. Cooper)

Hatch Beauchamp, with Elm Leigh (now the Old Rectory) in the foreground, *c.* 1908. Mr Bulpin lived here. Next door is Miss Taylor's Bay Cottage and then Charlie Steven's smithy. The shop in the distance was later run by County Stores and is now a private house. (J.F. Bridel)

Hatch post office, opposite Bickenhall Lane, *c.* 1930. The chapel can be seen in the distance.

The aptly named Farmers Arms at West Hatch, *c.* 1906. Some of these farm labourers are wearing knee bands, which were necessary to avoid constant friction and rapid wearing of the trouser knee. Mr Cridge, the landlord, is holding the child.

Hestercombe House, *c.* 1905. Viscount Portman acquired the house in 1872. Gertrude Jekyll's famous gardens, laid out between 1904 and 1909, have been restored by the County Council. Somerset Fire Brigade headquarters is now located here. (M. Cooper)

The funeral of Edward William Berkley Portman (b. 1856) in 1911. Edward William Berkley was the eldest son of eighty-two-year-old Lord Portman. The funeral cortège from Hestercombe to Cheddon Fitzpaine church was watched by hundreds of people. The coffin was carried on a large farm wagon drawn by a team of four horses. (M. Cooper)

Halse post office, *c.* 1910. This was sold in 1939 together with the Manor House, three farms, Halse Manor Mill, nineteen cottages and the village carpenter's shop. (Whitby)

Halse village street, viewed from outside Rock House, *c.* 1905. The first house on the left no longer exists but the thatched cottages remain. (M. Cooper)

Halse School, with most of the thirty-five children who attended, *c.* 1905. The school was given to the education authority when the estate was sold in 1939 by the young Lord of the Manor, Hugh Graham Evelyn Dunsterville. The date on the building is 1856.

The New Inn, Halse, run by Alfred Shawyer, *c.* 1905. On the right are Culver Cottages; the steps and doorway in the foreground no longer exist. Several of these Halse photos appear to have been taken at the same time, the same children having posed for the photographer in different parts of the village. (M. Cooper)

Halse, showing the gateway to Halse House, *c.* 1905. The building on the skyline is Manor Farm, home of the Greenway family. (M. Cooper)

West Monkton Street, *c.* 1954. On the right is R.F. and W.M. Marsh's post office stores. (F.W. Tarr)

A quiet corner in West Monkton, *c.* 1905. (Abraham)

SECTION TWO

West along the Tone

Mrs West and her daughter, Millie, outside the village shop in Norton Fitzwarren, *c.* 1920. The ices were home-made.

The Ring of Bells at Norton Fitzwarren, *c.* 1914.

Main Road and Spring Terrace (in the left distance), *c.* 1914. Both of these postcards were sold at Norton post office by Martha Critchard, who ran the business from around 1909 to 1916.

Station Road, Norton (*c.* 1909), on a postcard sold by Louisa Brennam at her drapers shop. Mr W.H. Brennam ran the post office after 1920.

Norton Fitzwarren post office and shop, *c.* 1920. (Chapman)

Fire at Home Place, Norton Fitzwarren, date unknown. The fire brigade at Norton was established in 1906 after the loan of an engine from Mr Arnold at the brewery.

The village club at Norton, *c.* 1905. The club building was erected in 1896 by Wilfred G. Marshall of Norton Manor at a cost of £1,000. Built of brick with Ham stone dressings, the building was enlarged by the addition of a bowling alley in 1897. (M. Cooper)

Norton Fitzwarren, view to the south, *c*. 1905. The enterprising photographer Mr Montague Cooper has climbed the church tower for this view. His work covered a large area of Somerset and he was probably the county's most prolific photographer.

Norton village, looking towards Taunton, *c*. 1906. The gentleman in the road is standing in front of what is now the chip shop. The thatched cottages in the distance (see p. 50) have since been pulled down.

Norton Fitzwarren coronation pageant, June 1911. After a dinner for 330 people at the village club a pageant, organized by Mr V.D. Stenhouse, was held on the lawn. (M. Cooper)

Norton coronation pageant, 1911. The village children and adults acted in seven episodes depicting local history. These included the Britons and the Romans, King Alfred, and Admiral Blake. Mr Moger and Mr Wise entertained everyone with their enormous doll costumes. (M. Cooper)

Children from Norton Fitzwarren School, c. 1925. They include Reg Sweeting, Frank Beak, Walter Ellis, Don Stutt, Chas Redwood, Ron Coles, Reg Brown, Lionel Ellis, Jack Redwood, Kathleen Porter, Alice Garland, Florence Ellis, May Bulgin, Edie Reed, Kathleen Eveleigh, Joyce Webber, Florence Lang, Dorothy Hembrow, Kathleen ?, Daisy Webber.

Norton Fitzwarren, *c.* 1904. The population in 1901 was 642, and the local people were proud of their ancient parish. It used to be said 'That Norton was a market town when Taunton was a furzy down.' (Crockett)

Norton village shop, with Norton Mills' chimney in the distance, *c.* 1904. The ancient cottages known as The Black Hole of Calcutta no longer exist. (Crockett)

Norton Fitzwarren, *c.* 1905. 'Monkey House' stands on the left; the roof was set alight by sparks from the brewery's steam wagon. The old chapel on the right was removed around 1940.

Chapel Cottages, next to the school, Norton, *c.* 1905. The chapel in the background was erected in 1821. (H.H. Hole)

Norton School, *c.* 1905. It was erected in 1872 and enlarged in 1901 to accommodate 120 children, and is now an Independent school. The little bell tower no longer exists. (H.H. Hole)

Old thatched cottages at Norton, *c.* 1904. These cottages can be seen in the background of the photograph on p. 45. Of the many thatched cottages that existed in the parish few, if any, remain. (Crockett)

Hillfarrance, *c.* 1909. This little village, well away from the main routes, has remained relatively unchanged. It now forms part of the parish of Oake.

Bradford on Tone, *c.* 1916. The church stands in the distance and the village shop near the centre. In the foreground is a KRIT car. Unkind critics claimed the name stood for 'Keeps Right in Town' but it was actually named after the American Kenneth Krittenden who introduced it in 1909. Like Ford, KRIT used vanadium steel for chassis components.

Bradford Mills, *c. 1905*. Mr W. Bird was the miller here at this time. There were several mills along the Tone including those at Bishops Hull, Fideoake, Langaller, Taunton and Bathpool. Most were involved in the production of flour. Many of the villages also had their own water-mills, including those at Bishops Lydeard, Trull, Pitminster, Combe Florey, Kingston, Creech St Michael, Staple Fitzpaine and Hatch Beauchamp. Some, like the recently restored mill at Trull, still retain their original machinery.

Bradford Bridge, *c.* 1902. 'In Ford and Ham and Ton the most of English names do run.' The name Bradford refers to a ford across the Tone near this point. (Brice)

Emma Rees serves 'Good Home Brewed Beer and Ale' at the Crown Inn, Rumwell, *c.* 1889. The ladies cycle appears to be a rather unorthodox design.

Hutcombe Café on Stonegallows Hill, *c.* 1935. The last recorded hanging at Stonegallows was of Thomas Gage, *alias* Torr, who had murdered his mistress with a hatchet at Goathurst in 1810.

'The Hutcombe Bunny', *c.* 1930. This postcard advertises bed and board at 13s 6d a day. Ushers Brewery Ltd converted the hotel to a modern steakhouse in 1965 at a cost of £6,000.

St Katharine's School, *c.* 1930. The school was founded at Clifton in 1892 by Mrs Meyrick Heath. It passed to the Woodard Society in 1918, who moved the school to Heatherton Park in May 1922. The Society added a sanatorium in 1923 and a chapel in 1928. A kindergarten and junior school opened in 1935. When the school closed in the 1950s it was catering for sixty boarders and ninety day-girls.

Bishops Hull Band, *c.* 1915. Unfortunately none of the players' names are known. (E.E. Cox)

Langaller Mills near Bishops Hull, *c.* 1905. The Gregory family owned this corn mill together with the mill at nearby Fideoake. The old lady with the shawl appears to be a wonderful country character. The small boy, standing just out of arm's reach, seems to have a great deal of respect for his 'granny'.

Langaller Mills, with members of the Gregory family, *c.* 1905. The boarded-up cottages in the foreground no longer exist nor, sadly, do the stately elms in the background. Somerset lost most of its mature elms to Dutch elm disease.

Bishops Hull Bridge Mill, *c.* 1905. Flour was ground at this mill until just prior to the First World War. The miller, named Mr Hutchings, did a very good trade with corn and meal. (Knight)

Tytherleigh Bridge and the mill at Bishops Hull, *c.* 1905. The foot-bridge across the Tone to Tytherleigh House and the mill weir have both been removed. (Wykeham)

Bishops Hull church and old vicarage, viewed from near the new school buildings, *c.* 1904. The vicarage was demolished in 1967 to make room for a church car park and hall. (Wykeham)

Shutewater Hill, Bishops Hull, *c.* 1905. A picture of Edwardian uniformity, although most of the cottages now have an identity of their own. Have the inhabitants had time to put on their Sunday best for the photographer? (Crockett)

Bishops Hull School was opened in Gypsy Lane in 1893. There were increasing problems with traffic on the nearby Wellington Road, and a new school opened opposite the manor in 1978.

Bishops Hull village, *c*. 1905. Mr Baker's bakery and the old thatched cob cottages were pulled down in 1911. It is a picturesque scene but conditions inside the cottages would have been poor. (Crockett)

Bishops Hull after redevelopment, *c*. 1912. The post office is in the centre. (Crockett)

Bishops Hull Manor, *c.* 1904. Colonel and Mrs De Cousey Rawlins lived here. When the Colonel's lady went by it was customary for the village girls to curtsey. Those who did not were usually scolded for their neglect. (Crockett)

Mr E. Horsey's Old Inn at Bishops Hull, *c.* 1904. The shopkeeper and some of the villagers stand outside the village shop. The rooms in the adjoining cottages were said to be so small and low you had to duck your head to enter. (Crockett)

Hanbury and Cotchings Boot Inn, at the top of Shutewater Hill, *c.* 1905. Mr Windle was the innkeeper at this time. One landlord of the inn was bandmaster of the village band, but he was said to have been as deaf as a post. (Crockett)

Bishops Hull, looking from the chapel towards Ivy Cottage, now the Meryan Hotel, *c.* 1906. Major Clarke, who lived here, gave the village children a pair of stockings and bag of sweets once a year.

Bishops Hull church from Netherclay Terrace, *c.* 1906. Miss Edith Trott's post office is second on the left. The parish of Bishops Hull included Rumwell, Upcott, Barr, Langaller, Long Run, Roughmoor, Fideoake and Galmington and in 1901 had a population of about eleven hundred.

Bishops Hull, looking towards Netherclay Terrace and the post office, *c.* 1904. The road ran around the corner and down the steep Fan Dance Hill to Tytherleigh Bridge over the River Tone. (Crockett)

St Peter's church, Bishops Hull, *c.* 1904. The New Inn on the right was run by Mrs E. Reen, and is now called The Cavalier. The old vicarage is in the background. (Frith)

Bishops Hull, *c.* 1905. New Inn Cottages were demolished around 1970. An old lady who lived here years ago took in washing at one old penny per dozen items.

Mountway Road, *c.* 1906. Smithy Cottages took their name from the old smithy which stood where the chip shop now stands. Mr Sully, the smith, was a kindly man who used to let the children warm their hands by his great fire.

Ken Rugg outside his house at Bishops Hull, *c.* 1930. Ken was born here in 1918.

A.H. Collard & Son's grocery shop, Bishops Hull, *c.* 1935. The card was written by Dennis Collard: 'This is my little shop and motor bike outside'. The Collards ran this shop and another in Corporation Street which was '99½ steps from the library'. The Bishops Hull shop closed in the early 1940s.

Richard Rudd's stores in the centre of Bishops Hull next to the thatched Old Inn, *c.* 1906. The shop has since been incorporated into the inn although it is still possible to trace its former position in the different brickwork. The girls and boys in the village street are wearing traditional clothes. It was not always easy to differentiate between the sexes because younger boys sometimes wore an older sister's outgrown clothes. This state of affairs seems to have been accepted without the unfortunate boy being subject to ridicule.

Bishops Hull Church.

A classic Bishops Hull photograph from the Francis Frith Company; unusually the original negative still survives. This postcard, published around 1905, shows the arrival of the milk delivery cart. The man behind the double door is Charlie Richards. He would play his concertina to all who cared to stop and listen and the village children would dance around his doorstep. Part of the premises survives as The Cavalier Inn (ex New Inn) (see p. 64) where people can still find musical entertainment to this day.

SECTION THREE
East along the Tone

Floods at Creech St Michael in 1910. This photograph was taken from the church tower looking towards the old canal embankment. (J.G. Mitchell)

Ruishton Inn, *c.* 1905.

Ruishton church, *c.* 1905. The old cottages between Drakes Farm and the church have been demolished. (Abraham)

The Tone Bridge at Creech, *c.* 1905. The original bridge, believed to have been a timber structure on stone piers, was replaced around 1800 by the stone bridge. In 1848 Edward Murch of Bridgwater removed the parapets and replaced them with iron girders and railings. (M. Cooper)

A typical swing bridge on the Taunton and Bridgwater canal at Creech, *c.* 1904. The 14½ mile canal was completed in 1827 at a cost of £71,000. In 1867 the Bridgwater and Exeter Railway bought the canal and the last commercial traffic ran in 1907. (W.T. Brass)

Revd William Shillito addressing the crowd at Creech St Michael bazaar, *c.* 1904. The village constable, Thomas Osmont, keeps order among the younger members of the crowd in the background. (W.T. Brass)

The Stocks in Creech Churchyard.

The stocks in Creech churchyard, *c.* 1904; another set with an odd number of holes.

Creech North End, with Laurel Villa on the left, *c.* 1905. The cottages in the centre are no longer there.

Creech Heathfield, *c.* 1905. Northend Farm is on the left. Both of these photographs were taken by Montague Cooper from almost the same viewpoint and probably at the same time.

POST OFFICE, CREECH ST MICHAEL. 840.

The post office, Bell Inn and smithy at Creech St Michael, *c.* 1905. William Francis ran the post office where he also traded as a draper and grocer. The smithy was run by the Stevens family. Mr B. Stevens took over the smithy in 1920 and ran it until 1935. Because there was no local dentist he also drew teeth with a special tool he had made. Sensible folk availing themselves of this service made a prior visit to the Bell Inn and arrived for treatment well fortified with brandy. The Bell Inn dates to before 1824. In the late nineteenth century it belonged to the Stogumber Brewery who were taken over by the West Somerset Brewery at Taunton. In 1897 Arnold and Sons (later Arnold and Hancock) acquired the property and they in turn were bought by Ushers Brewery Ltd in 1955.

Creech Paper Mill, *c.* 1910. The mill opened in 1876 (the chimney bears the date 1875). It was originally owned by R. Sommerville but was taken over by Purnells in 1946. The British Printing Corporation took over the site in 1965.

Bathpool garage and Imperial tea-rooms, *c.* 1930. At about this time ownership passed from Richard Matthews to Dyer & Crofts.

The Bathpool road, photographed from the approach to the railway bridge, *c.* 1908. The large pits, dug to construct the bridge approaches, were filled up with town rubbish in the 1890s. The largest pit and part of the field were excavated in 1992 to form a lake, as part of the riverside development.

The Bathpool Inn and the main road into Taunton, *c.* 1905. (Abraham)

Bathpool Mills, *c.* 1905. The premises had been partially rebuilt after a serious fire around 1890. (Tuck)

Bathpool Mills, from the GWR main railway line, *c.* 1910. Passengers along this route had a grandstand view of the fire which occurred in 1915. (J.G. Mitchell)

Thomas J. Redler and Sons, Bathpool Mills, c. 1900. The installation of a portable steam-engine has improved the traditional water driven process. A second serious fire at these premises in September 1915 highlighted a curious dispute. Taunton Fire Brigade, raised by the fire alarm, sat helplessly by on the town boundary as the premises were gutted. A working agreement between the Borough and Rural District Councils had been suspended, which meant that the Borough Fire Brigade was unable to attend rural fires. Unfortunately, the mill was just outside the Borough, although it is likely that the fire brigade would have been of little help such was the intensity of the blaze. The spectacle drew crowds from miles around.

SECTION FOUR

On the Moors

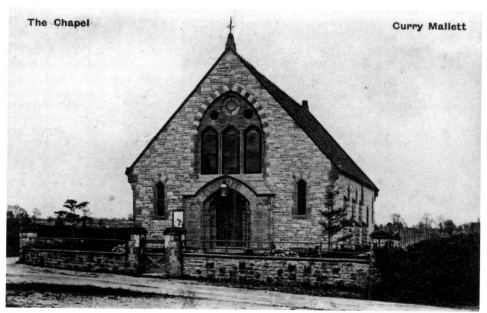

The Baptist chapel, Curry Mallet, *c*. 1906. The chapel was built in 1773–4 on Duchy of Cornwall land acquired from the Prince of Wales at a cost of £620.

Lyng from the church tower, *c.* 1905. The Rose and Crown on the left remains but the cottages on the right have been replaced by newer houses. (J.G. Mitchell)

Curry Mallet, *c.* 1910. Job Viles' bakers cart passes the home of Sarah Keates. The bakehouse is the thatched building on the right and Stud Farm is in the background. (J.F. Bridel)

Thomas Giblett's shop, North Curry. The poster in the window of the shop in London House is dated 1906. Thomas Giblett started his grocery business in North Curry around 1889 when he took over the established business of F. Coombes. Fashions at this time were fairly uniform, the boys and girls in this photo are dressed as in any other contemporary scene.

Village green, North Curry, *c.* 1940. At the end of Church Road is Gillards Ironmongers advertising BSA bicycles.

The 'smallest cinema in England' opened in Moor Lane, North Curry in the early 1950s. It was run by Ken Mapledoram and called The Bijou.

The Pavement and post office, North Curry, *c*. 1950.

Jubilee Square, North Curry, *c*. 1950. George Hutchings stands outside his shop, now run by his two sons, Ken and Mike. The building behind the car is the Bird in Hand Inn.

North Curry post office, *c*. 1905. The Victorian Jubilee monument stands in the foreground. This postcard was published by James Beel who ran the post office between 1883 and 1910.

Moredon, North Curry, *c*. 1905. This was the home of Major William Barret, High Sheriff of Somerset. (T. Giblett)

Carriages at North Curry, *c.* 1905. The gas lamp was removed when the First World War memorial was erected. The building in the background bears the name the Old Brewery.

CHRISTMAS

GREETINGS.

Another busy scene in North Curry, *c.* 1905. This postcard was sold in Thomas Giblett's shop in London House, left.

The Grange, North Curry, *c.* 1905. It stood on the corner of the road to Stoke St Gregory. (Crockett)

North Curry, *c.* 1903. At this time Thomas Giblett occupied the premises later used by George Hutchings. On the far left is James Bradbeer's bakery and sweet-shop. (Abraham)

Jubilee Monument, North Curry.

The Jubilee monument, North Curry, with the Old Brewery in the background, *c.* 1905. (T. Giblett)

Church Avenue, North Curry, *c.* 1908. The avenue of elms to 'The Cathedral in the Moor' was damaged by gales in March 1910, and subsequent deterioration led to all the trees being cut down. (C.A.S. Co.)

Victoria Terrace, North Curry, *c.* 1940. The ivy-covered building is the manse but by 1943 the ivy had been removed. (Tuck)

A view from the Old Brewery, North Curry, *c.* 1904. Queen's House, behind the tree, housed Dare's Bakery in later years. The thatched cottage, left, now has a tiled roof. (M. Cooper)

A distant view of North Curry showing the parish church of St Peter and St Paul, *c.* 1905. North Curry was a large parish with a population of 1,525 in 1901. Included in the parish were Newport, Wrantage, Lillesdon and Knapp. (M. Cooper)

The Methodist chapel, North Curry, *c.* 1905. The building was erected in 1833. Windmill Hill leads to Taunton in the distance.

Wrantage post office near North Curry, *c.* 1905. Mr William Goss was sub-postmaster and draper at these premises. He was also a deacon and church treasurer at Hatch Baptist chapel. The Chard canal ran through the village close to the post office to enter the 500 yd long Crimson Hill tunnel just outside the village. The bargees used to lie on the barges and 'walk' them through the tunnel. (G.C. Fisher)

Floods at Stoke St Gregory, 1929. This view is towards Athelney Crossing with Arthur Patten's Athelney Stores on the left. The Railway Hotel is now the Pigeons. The building in the centre housed Sonner Woodland's pony and trap.

Curload floods, 1929. Withygrove House is on the left, Ivy House to the right. The traditional industry of withy-growing and basket-making is still carried on in the area. Nobody was hurt in the flooding but a railway worker fell into a ditch and drowned shortly after.

Meare Green just outside Stoke St Gregory, *c.* 1905. On the left is Box Cottage and beyond this Holly Farm.

Slough Lane, the road from Stoke St Gregory to Stathe, *c.* 1906. In the foreground is the entrance to Slough Farm (now Court). The cart is coming down the lane from Dykes Farm on the hilltop.

SECTION FIVE

Beneath the Quantocks

POST OFFICE
THURLOXTON. 184.

Thurloxton post office on a postcard dated 1909. The writer states that this is the first postcard of the village.

Westhay, on the Broomfield Road out of Kingston, *c.* 1910. This was the home of Isaac Badcock KC, MA, JP. (M. Cooper)

Kingston St Mary, *c.* 1905. Nearly nine hundred people lived in the parish at this time. The parish church of St Mary is in the distance. There was a chapel at Greenway and a National School run by Mr and Mrs Bunston. (M. Cooper)

'Bird's-eye view' of Kingston St Mary, c. 1915. Frank Stoaling was licensee of the Swan Inn in the foreground, and also ran popular motor brake excursions to the Quantocks during the First World War.

Church Road, Kingston St Mary, c. 1905. The oak tree was planted by Miss E.B. Cheetham of Tetton House on 13 December 1897 to celebrate Queen Victoria's Diamond Jubilee. The parish rooms were built where the wooden fence stands, the former site of Hunts Cottage, in 1923. (Abraham)

The shop, left, at Kingston St Mary, *c*. 1905. A shop and post office still occupy this site and at the time of writing there are still a couple of enamel signs remaining on the wall. (Abraham)

Kingston Manor House, *c*. 1904. At this time it was the home of His Majesty's Inspector of Schools Mr J.A. Willis. (M. Cooper)

Kingston St Mary, photographed from the corner of Lodes Lane, *c.* 1905. (M. Cooper)

Kingston St Mary, looking down the hill towards the stores, *c.* 1938. Near where the car is parked a shop sign, 'A. Bulgin, Poulterer', still exists in the wall, and is dated to the late 1940s.

Kingston stores with Albert Boddy's bakery next door, c. 1920. The two shops have now been incorporated into a single shop called the Old Bakery. There are some fine enamel signs along the garden wall which was probably erected more as a fence than for advertising purposes. This 'street jewellery' is quite collectable now. When we were children we used to throw stones at the signs and watch the enamel 'ping' off. At one time signs could be found on old shed roofs and around allotment compost heaps but this is rarely the case nowadays.

The 107 ft tower of St Mary's church, Bishops Lydeard, *c.* 1905. The view is towards Church Street. The two girls are standing at the entrance to Mr C.W. Barrett's Brookside at the end of Mount Street. (M. Cooper)

The Taunton road, Bishops Lydeard, *c.* 1935. James Pihlen's garage is on the left and the Lethbridge Arms in the distance.

Mount Street, Bishop Lydeard, *c.* 1904. The village school run by Mr and Mrs Simons is on the right. (M. Cooper)

Mount Street, Bishops Lydeard, *c.* 1915. This part of the street used to be called Frog Street. The cottage on the left has been built on the site of some old cottages which burnt down in 1906 (see p. 102). (M. Cooper)

Frog Street, Bishops Lydeard, after the fire on Monday 9 April 1906. The fire began at 4.30 p.m. in the roof of the cottage at the west end of the row. Bishops Lydeard and Taunton Fire Brigades fought the blaze until midnight but the whole row of seven cottages was gutted. Nobody was hurt and everybody managed to rescue most of their possessions. (Crockett)

The Lethbridge Arms Hotel, formerly the Gore Inn, c. 1910. In the inn car park is a well-preserved Fives wall surmounted by a Dutch gable.

Frog Street, Bishops Lydeard, *c.* 1904. The row of seven old cottages on the left, just beyond the garden of Warre House, was gutted by fire in April 1906. Taunton Fire Brigade, summoned by telegram, arrived after only thirty-two minutes. The motor car is the photographer's own 12 hp Belgica. (M. Cooper)

Frog Street, *c.* 1910. This section of road between Gore Square and Mount Street was so called because it often flooded.

St Mary Street, now High Street, Bishops Lydeard, *c.* 1905. On the right, constructed of local red sandstone, are the almshouses built by Sir Richard Grobham in 1616. (M. Cooper)

Mary Street, *c.* 1925. George Axe's saddle and harness shop is on the left. The pole at the junction of West Street is a converted tramways standard from Taunton and is still standing. (R.A.P. Co.)

Bishops Lydeard, photographed from the church tower, *c.* 1905. This view is towards the south with the school on the left. The Lethbridge Arms is in the far distance, right. (M. Cooper)

Bishops Lydeard, *c.* 1905. Another lofty view from the church looking towards Cothelstone. The Independent chapel is in the middle distance and the grounds of Lydeard House on the left. (M. Cooper)

Van Heusen's factory at Bishops Lydeard. The factory opened on the site of the old wagon works in the early 1950s. On the opening day company executives toured the premises. The lady second from the left is Ethel Langford who was the personnel officer. John Van Heusen had invented the new, more comfortable, semi-stiff collar in America, and the collars were first manufactured in England in Taunton's Viney Street factory in 1922. Initially employing twenty-three people the company became one of the town's biggest employers.

Mr T.A. Hembrow of Wick Farm, Bishops Lydeard, stands proudly with his prize cattle, winners of Third Prize at Taunton Christmas Fat Stock Show in 1907. This postcard was used as an advertisement for Calthrop's 'Lucky Star' animal cakes and meals. (Calthrop)

Combe Florey School, *c.* 1905. At this time it was run by Thomas Lilley and his wife. The school was built around 1848 and subsequently enlarged to accommodate seventy children. The building is now a private house. (M. Cooper)

Combe Florey, *c.* 1906. On the left is the village shop run by Miss Matilda Trebble. The buildings still remain today.

Combe Florey ford from the Minehead Road, *c.* 1906. The ford has long since been replaced by a road bridge. It is tempting to believe the horse in the field is a montage added by the photographer for artistic reasons. (M. Cooper)

Lydeard St Lawrence, *c.* 1905. This view up the hill shows Court Farm on the left. The house on the right is St Bees which is now obscured from this view by the later Pond House. The village grocery shop is in the centre. (M. Cooper)

Victoria Terrace, Lydeard St Lawrence, *c.* 1908. There is a gap now where the sideways-on house stands. The site of the old thatched cottage has been redeveloped.

Beneath the Blackdowns

Pitminster post office, *c.* 1920. The road on the right leads to Blagdon Hill.

Pitminster, *c.* 1904. Pitminster House is on the left and the old corn mill stream (now filled in) leads to the corn mill in the distance. There has been a mill in this vicinity since 1086. (Abraham)

The mill-pond, Pitminster, *c.* 1910. The pond was situated at the head of the mill stream above but has since been filled in.

Miss Joan Upham, sub-postmistress, stands in the doorway of the village post office at Pitminster, *c*. 1910. The building was damaged by fire in 1955 and Mr and Mrs Lee, the occupants, lived in the two habitable rooms while a new house was built beside it. Mrs Lee had attended the school in 1906 and could remember the headmaster, Mr Sparkes, who was well respected and a strict disciplinarian. In 1911, after fourteen years at Pitminster, Mr Sparkes succeeded Harry Whale at Trull School. An illustrated history of the old school was published in 1981 in aid of the restoration fund.

Pitminster church, dedicated to St Andrew and St Mary, together with the rectory.

The school, Pitminster, *c.* 1905. The school was built in the Parish Orchard in 1840 and when it opened it catered for 101 children on weekdays and 97 on Sundays. Numbers declined to forty-three by 1913 and the school finally closed in 1921 after which it was used as a village club. During the Second World War the building returned to its original use when it was used by 45 evacuee children from Plaistow. It is now used for a variety of purposes. (M. Cooper)

Barton Grange, *c.* 1905. Only one wing now remains of this house built by Humphrey Colles in Tudor times. The house was reduced in size at the beginning of the nineteenth century and further reduced in 1931. The Corfe–Pitminster parish boundary runs right through the building. (Abraham)

Sellicks Green, Blagdon, *c.* 1910. The Pitminster road leads off to the right. A smithy occupied the buildings on the left in the background.

Taunton Corporation's reservoirs, Blagdon Hill, *c.* 1920. The construction of a fourth reservoir began at Quants near Lowton but the project was abandoned before completion. Tunnels were driven through the hill to bring water into the reservoir.

Luxhay reservoir in 1905. The opening ceremony has been completed (see p. 155) and the reservoir is filling up. (Chaffin)

Fulwood Farm, *c.* 1910. This building, on the road to Blagdon, now has a tiled roof. Mrs Bessie Sparks is standing outside. The farm was run by Walter Sparks from around 1903.

Samuel Shire's smithy at Blagdon, *c.* 1915. An anvil hangs above the door and a poster advertises a furniture sale at Wilton Grove.

Blagdon Hill post office, *c.* 1928. The men standing in the road are postmen.

Blagdon Hill, looking north, *c.* 1905. On the left is the White Lion serving 'Hanbury and Cotchings Fine Ales'. William Warren ran the inn together with his wheelwrights business.

Blagdon Hill post office, *c.* 1905. Mrs Selina Wescombe, the sub-postmistress, is in the doorway.

Blagdon Hill, looking north, *c.* 1905. In the doorway of the Lamb and Flag, right, stand Mrs Loman and her young son, Frankie. The Mission Room is just behind them.

Blagdon Hill, from the Mission Room porch, c. 1910. Blagdon House is on the left. The narrower section of road no longer exists. (Miers)

Blagdon Hill, looking up the village street from the post office, c. 1905. The vehicle is possibly the carrier's cart. (Senior)

Blagdon village, *c.* 1906. A quiet scene on what is now a busy road. Julia Cottage, left, bears the date 1837. The small boy is playing with an iron hoop fashioned, perhaps, by the local blacksmith. Blagdon Hill together with Lowton, Staplehay and Eastbrook formed part of the parish of Pitminster. The population density in 1901 was fairly low – 1,262 people lived in an area of 5,274 acres. There were schools at Pitminster and Blagdon and chapels at Fulwood, Chelmsine and Blagdon. Prior to the arrival of the motor bus, *Lady Betty*, four carriers ran from Blagdon to Taunton on Wednesdays and Saturdays.

Blagdon Hill, looking south, *c.* 1920. The building in the distance is the Mission Room which was built in 1878. Blagdon Green is the open area of ground on the left.

Walter Dyer stands outside his bakery at Blagdon Hill, *c.* 1905. The same building, now substantially modernized, can be seen beyond the smithy on p. 115.

The Lamb and Flag Inn at Blagdon Hill, *c.* 1905. The licensee at this time was James Fry Loman.

Angersleigh Court, on a postcard written by Annie ('our house'), *c.* 1908. Leigh Court was built soon after 1829 and was home to Arthur Edgell Eastwood JP from around 1900 for many years. (His car is in the photograph on p. 22.)

Poundisford Park, *c.* 1906. The park was built shortly after 1546 by William Hill, son of Roger Hill of Poundisford Lodge. Amy has written this postcard 'of our lovely home'. Living here in 1906 was Bishop Moorhouse MD, the late Bishop of Manchester.

Lowton post office with staff and postman, *c.* 1906.

Lowton post office, *c.* 1908. The Mapledoram family ran the post office and shop for over forty years.

Lowton post office, after the cottage next door had burnt down, *c.* 1950. The post office closed around the mid-1970s.

Corfe village, *c.* 1910. The post office is in the last building on the right. The building on the left is the village smithy. A film made about the smith, Bill Bosley, was shown extensively in the district.

Starkey Knight and Ford's White Hart Inn at Corfe, *c.* 1920. The road on the right leads to Pitminster. (R.A.P. Co.)

Brook Farm, Corfe, *c*. 1920. It was the home of the Bond family for many years. (R.A.P. Co.)

Old cottages by the church in Corfe, *c*. 1905. It seems possible to transport oneself back ninety years in time as this view is almost identical today. Although the thatch is a little worn and the wall not quite so neat, these old cottages have stood the test of time very well. (Crockett)

Corfe, showing the end of the cottages on the previous page, *c.* 1905. The village church is in the distance. From 1898 the church was lit by electricity powered by a dynamo installed by the churchwarden, Francis Newton, founder of Newtons Electrical Works in Taunton in 1891. (Abraham)

Corfe, looking south, *c.* 1905. The school building, right, accommodated ninety children from Corfe and Orchard Portman. It is now a private house. (Abraham)

Corfe Vicarage and School, *c.* 1904. The village war memorial now stands where the elm tree used to be. The photographer's M.M.C. 9 hp motor car, registration number Y308, is in the distance. Mr Cooper also had a 2-seater De Dion registered Y94 in 1903 and the Belgica seen on p.102. (M. Cooper)

Corfe village looking north from outside the White Hart Inn, *c.* 1904. (M. Cooper)

Corfe village, looking south, *c.* 1905. The Baptist chapel on the left was built in 1897. (M. Cooper)

Staple Fitzpaine, *c.* 1905. In 1944 nearly all of the parish was sold to the Crown Land Commissioners by Lady Portman to pay death duties. Of over 20,000 acres only the Manor House and 40 acres remained in the hands of Lady Portman. After a thousand years of existence under a local Lord of the Manor almost all the land and cottages now belonged to some unknown gentlemen in London. (Abraham)

SECTION SEVEN

The Railway

An engine chugs gamely through the floods at Creech St Michael, *c.* 1890. The paper-mills are behind the windmill on the left. After quadrupling, this section of line became Creech Halt in 1928. (Brice)

Hatch station in winter, *c.* 1908. This Up view shows the engine shed and signal box. The school is just visible on the skyline above the shed. (J.F. Bridel)

Hatch station, *c.* 1905. The station building, constructed of brick with freestone facings, is shown in this Up view. The track has been laid on longitudinal sleepers. (M. Cooper)

An Up view towards the 154 yd long Hatch tunnel at Hatch station, *c.* 1905. This was the only tunnel on the 13 mile branch line which ran from Creech Junction to Chard Junction. The line opened in 1866 and was constructed so that it could be doubled in the future, although this was never done.

A Down view, Hatch station, *c.* 1905. The complete branch line was converted to standard gauge on Sunday 19 July 1891 in only twenty hours. It was closed to passenger traffic in 1962 and finally closed to goods traffic in 1964.

Creech St Michael Halt, *c.* 1930. This opened to passengers in 1928 and at that time a third-class single fare into Taunton was 4d. In 1938 and 1939 the station won the Exeter District special award for the best platform gardens. The main attractions were the dazzling borders lovingly tended by the porters in charge, Mr H.C. Hobbs and Mr F.T. Haydon.

Creech Halt, looking towards the road bridge, *c.* 1930. The station closed in 1964 and was demolished in 1969.

Thornfalcon station, *c.* 1906. The station was opened in 1871 and closed in 1962. Stone from the local quarries was distributed from here by G. Small of Taunton on the branch line to Chard.

Thornfalcon station shortly after closure in 1962. Evidently the original timber platform had been replaced by one of concrete.

The Cape Mail Express was wrecked at Norton Fitzwarren in 1890. The express had ploughed into a goods engine at 60 mph. Ten people were killed and nine injured. Notice the dual gauge track which was finally converted to standard gauge in 1892. A London evening paper reporting the accident and a society wedding transposed the two captions 'A Terrible Disaster' and 'An Interesting Event'! (Petherick)

Norton Fitzwarren railway crash, 1940. Almost exactly fifty years to the day later, the second great Norton Fitzwarren railway disaster occurred. The Paddington–Penzance express hauled by *King George VI* was wrecked in November 1940.

Two more photographs of the Norton accident, 1940. The London driver of GWR 6028 *King George VI* moved his train on to the relief line to allow a mail train to pass. His intention was to rejoin the main line on crossover points at Norton. The express driver mistook the main line green signals as his own and after building up speed to 40 mph realized too late that he was still on the relief line.

The Norton accident, 1940. No. 6028 careered through the catch points at the end of the relief line and half buried itself in the soft soil, hurling its thirteen carriages across all four lines. The fireman was killed but the driver survived.

The coaches were very badly damaged. Twenty-seven passengers were killed and over seventy injured. Many were servicemen. The mail train had missed the derailment by just a few seconds, thus avoiding an even more horrific accident.

A battered *King George VI* at Taunton station, November 1940. Although it also appears in *Taunton in Old Photographs* I have included this photograph here to complete the sequence. After its first publication I received a letter from Mr Fear which told the story of this photograph. Despite strict security Mr Fear and Mr Thomas, both railway employees, decided to have a close look at the engine. They smuggled a camera into the engine shed in a Reed and Giles fishmongers bag which also contained overalls and a mackintosh. The hastily taken photograph is the one that appears above. (D. Fear)

Norton Fitzwarren station, *c.* 1905. Originally on the Bristol and Exeter Railway it was adopted by the Great Western Railway in 1878. The station opened in 1873, was modified in the early 1930s and closed in 1961. There is a fine enamel sign for the Anglo–Bavarian Brewery who changed their name to the Anglo Brewing Company around 1914.

A long Up view at Norton station, *c.* 1906. The branch line to Minehead leads off in the foreground.

Norton Fitzwarren station after the line had been quadrupled and two island platforms had replaced the original layout. The 131 lever signal-box is on the right.

A goods train derailment at Durston in 1908 when about twelve trucks went off the line near Cogload Junction. The engine farthest right is a 388 class locomotive No. 274 with a Swindon boiler in 1906 livery. (M. Cooper)

Durston, 1908. A 10 ton hand crane on a six-wheeled chassis lifts a truck back on to the track. The use of this crane indicates that nothing heavier than trucks had to be lifted. (M. Cooper)

Durston, 1908. Workmen clear the track of debris. (M. Cooper)

An Up view, Bishops Lydeard station, *c.* 1907. The station had opened in 1862 and the construction of the line had been one of I.K. Brunel's last projects. He died in 1859.

A Down view, Bishops Lydeard station, *c.* 1907. A passing loop and the Up platform on the right were constructed in 1906. On the left is the conveniently located goods shed with cattle pens in the foreground.

An Up view, Bishops Lydeard station, *c. 1962*. British Rail closed the station in 1971 to form the Eastern terminus of the privately owned West Somerset Railway.

Bishops Lydeard station, looking across to the Down platform and goods shed, *c. 1962*. The station was the scene of some excitement in September 1915 when the royal train stayed overnight. The village schoolchildren attended and sang three verses of 'God Save the King' to a delighted monarch.

SECTION EIGHT

Transport

Lipton's delivery cart with canine driver somewhere in the Curry Rivel area. (W. Linton)

The inaugural run of the motor bus *Lady Betty* in May 1914. The bus was photographed at the Stapley home of Mr Ireland, the proprietor. A good crowd turned out to witness the arrival of the bus, including Mr A.C. Allen and Mr Mynors representing Allen & Son who had supplied the vehicle second-hand. The bus seated twenty people and could carry a large amount of baggage. She ran regularly from Taunton to Churchstanton serving Corfe and Pitminster although Blagdon Hill proved to be a severe test on many occasions. (Crockett)

Thomas Penny's delivery cart outside the New Inn at Fitzhead, *c.* 1906.

Sam Wine, the founder of Wine's Taxis, delivering a circular saw frame manufactured by Allen & Son of Taunton.

Mrs Eland Clatworthy presents a smart turnout at Cutsey near Trull, *c.* 1910. (M. Cooper)

Pony and trap outside W. Jennings' Bell Hotel at Bishops Lydeard. The writer of this postcard, stamped April 1908, points out that it has only just been issued. (Crockett)

W.C. Shute's delivery van, a common sight in the Taunton area in the early 1950s.

Creech St Michael, *c.* 1925. Even the floods did not stop the milkman from completing his round. The resourceful Mr Witcombe of Priory Park Dairy employed a boat to reach his stranded customers.

An early motor caravan at the Peacock Guest House, Adsborough, *c.* 1930.

The Royal Mail van at Williton. This is probably an early version of the Lacre O type lorry introduced in 1909. Note the rear axle chain transmission. Allen's of Taunton had the contract to supply and maintain these vehicles. (H.H. Hole)

Norton Mills' van, accompanied by Len Webber and Jack Hodge, *c*. 1915.

Norton Mills' horse transport, *c*. 1905.

A self-moving traction-engine at a timber works near Bishops Lydeard. Machinery such as this did much to reduce the hard manual labour of working the land. In the old days timber was cut by hand across a saw pit, the man in the pit being constantly showered by sawdust.

Mr Beach has arrived in his car at an unknown location, *c.* 1904. A 1,000 mile endurance rally in 1900 had introduced the motor car to many rural folk. (H. Stainer)

Members of Taunton Motor Club at the Pines Café on Buncombe Hill, *c.* 1936. The club organized regular hill climbs on the Quantocks between the wars.

The perils of early motoring. The front wheel assembly on early motor cars was easily damaged. Mr Beach's motor engineers have arrived to offer assistance. The photograph dates to after January 1904 when national registration became compulsory.

Another motor mishap. On this occasion the damage is rather more extensive and a lorry has been called to collect the wreck. (M. Cooper)

SECTION NINE

People

Members of the Girls' Friendly Society with their caravan near Taunton, *c.* 1916. The Society was formed to promote Christian beliefs and was particularly active during the First World War. Two hundred members attended their annual festival at Taunton in July 1915. (M. Cooper)

Edward Vincent ('Eddie') Beach on his 1927 AJS 350cc OHV motorcycle at the
Shoreditch grass track in 1936. Eddie joined the Taunton Motor Club in 1919 and won
the first of many trophies in 1923. The firm of James Beach & Co. was formed in 1873
and the family were foremost in promoting the use of the motor car in Taunton in the
early 1900s.

Opening ceremony at Luxhay Reservoir, Blagdon, June 1905. The reservoir was 57 ft deep and covered 17 acres when full. The ceremony was conducted by Councillor Josiah Lewis, Mayor of Taunton. The gentleman at the centre, bottom row, with his hand in his pocket, is Mr Van Trump, who became Mayor of Taunton during the First World War.

Scythesmen Giles, Mead, Collins and Burt with Tom Tucker and collie Clover at Hatch Hollow on the Curry Mallet road, *c.* 1905. Each man carries a sharpening stone. The fastest mower took the lead and the rest had to keep up at 3 yd intervals. A good scythesman could mow 3 acres of corn a day. Grass was much harder; a single acre a day was a very high output.

Haymaking at North End, Creech St Michael, *c.* 1922. The farm belonged to Wilfred Knight who bought this 22 hp Fordson tractor in 1920. The cart was made by local carpenter Francis Poole. Also present are Mrs Dorcas Knight and Mr William Pendry (with pitchfork). (Mitchell)

Edward, Prince of Wales, on one of several visits to the Duchy estate at Curry Mallet, *c.* 1930. The Prince is meeting Mr Herbert Paul and other Duchy tenants at Manor Farm. At an earlier visit on 19 July 1923 the Prince visited Park Farm and Bartletts Farm.

Harvest supper, Lowton village hall, *c.* 1946. The principal guests were Commander Dorien Smith and Archdeacon Fitch.

Threshing at Curry Mallet, *c.* 1902. The man on the traction-engine is George Mico who died in 1906 aged 27. The owner of the engine and threshing-machine, Samuel J. Perry of Curry Mallet, is standing in front of the traction-engine. The steam-engine drives the threshing-machine and the threshed grain is loaded into bags. Normally the bag weights were 12 stone for oats and 16 stone for barley or wheat. The two men on the threshing-machine are the feeder and band cutter. The men with the pitchforks forked sheaves from the corn stack on to the machine. This had to be done in a precise manner with the ears lying in the same direction. A regular rhythm of work had to be kept up and at the end of the day the machinery was moved on to the next job. The work was long and tiring, usually starting at 4 a.m. when the threshing men had to rise to get the steam up.

Hatch Beauchamp Observer Corps at their post, Y2, in 1942. Those present include W. Caunter, W. Yeo, W. Allen, E. Bailey, M. Denman, R. Huxtable, T. Duke, L. Newman, F. Wensley, G. Stevens, B. Morgan, W. Keates, A. Hardwill, G. Court, A. Jennings, S. Quick, A. Davis, A. Govier, E. Jeffrey, J. Mole, P. Mico.

Shoreditch grass track, 1936. The motorcyclists are, left to right: W. Colman, Eddie Beach, D.H. Baker, W. Spurrell and J.H. Benton-Scott.

Acknowledgements

After the publication of *Taunton in Old Photographs* it seemed only natural that a companion volume of the local villages should follow. Such is the scarcity of photographs of this small rural area that the author has taken over fifteen years to accumulate sufficient material for this book. When it comes to photographic records towns are fairly well catered for but photographs of villages are rare.

None the less, these village photographs tell us a good deal more about life in Somerset at the turn of the century than their urban counterparts. The village was a true community where everyone had their place in the local order of things. Nearly every village had its own post office to cater for communications, its own shop to cater for material needs and knowledge of wider events and its own school and places of worship. There was little need to travel far.

Now all these things have changed, villages are no longer self-sufficient in their needs and the community spirit has long since departed. No doubt people worked harder, endured more privation and had less leisure time. Despite this one cannot help feeling that country people had a greater awareness of nature and the meaning of life. If these photographs can rekindle just a little of that awareness then the author would be well satisfied with his efforts.

The following people have rendered the author assistance in the preparation of this book for which he is profoundly grateful:

Mr Berry, Bill Board, Miss L. Brannam, Mr A. Bridel, David Bromwich (at the Local History Library), Les Cleal, Mrs J. Colmer, Mr Daly, Margaret Dickson, Mr Len Doble, Mr D. Fear, Pat and Fred Gamblin, Mr and Mrs B. Harse, Miss Olivia Hunter, Mr M. Hutchings, Miss Long (deceased), Mrs M. Oaten, Mrs M. Palmer, Mr Robin Parker of the Taunton Camera Centre, Mr M. Pendry, Ken and Bron Rugg, Somerset Record Office Staff, Ray and Pat Sparks, Mr W.T.C. Stephens, Mrs Warren, Mike White, Ernie Wide, John Yendall.

I have taken every care in the verification of the facts presented in this book. However, even contemporary records of events can contain errors and if any errors do occur in the text then I must apologize. If readers would like to contribute towards my knowledge of the photographs and events in these pages, or if they have any similar material I could study, I hope they will contact me.